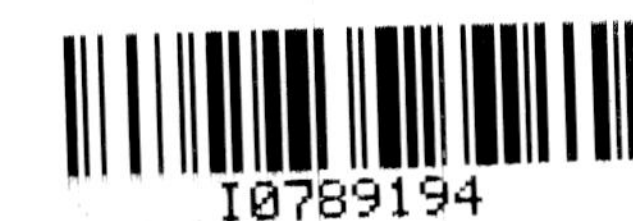

THIS BOOK

BELONGS TO:

COLOR TEST PAGE

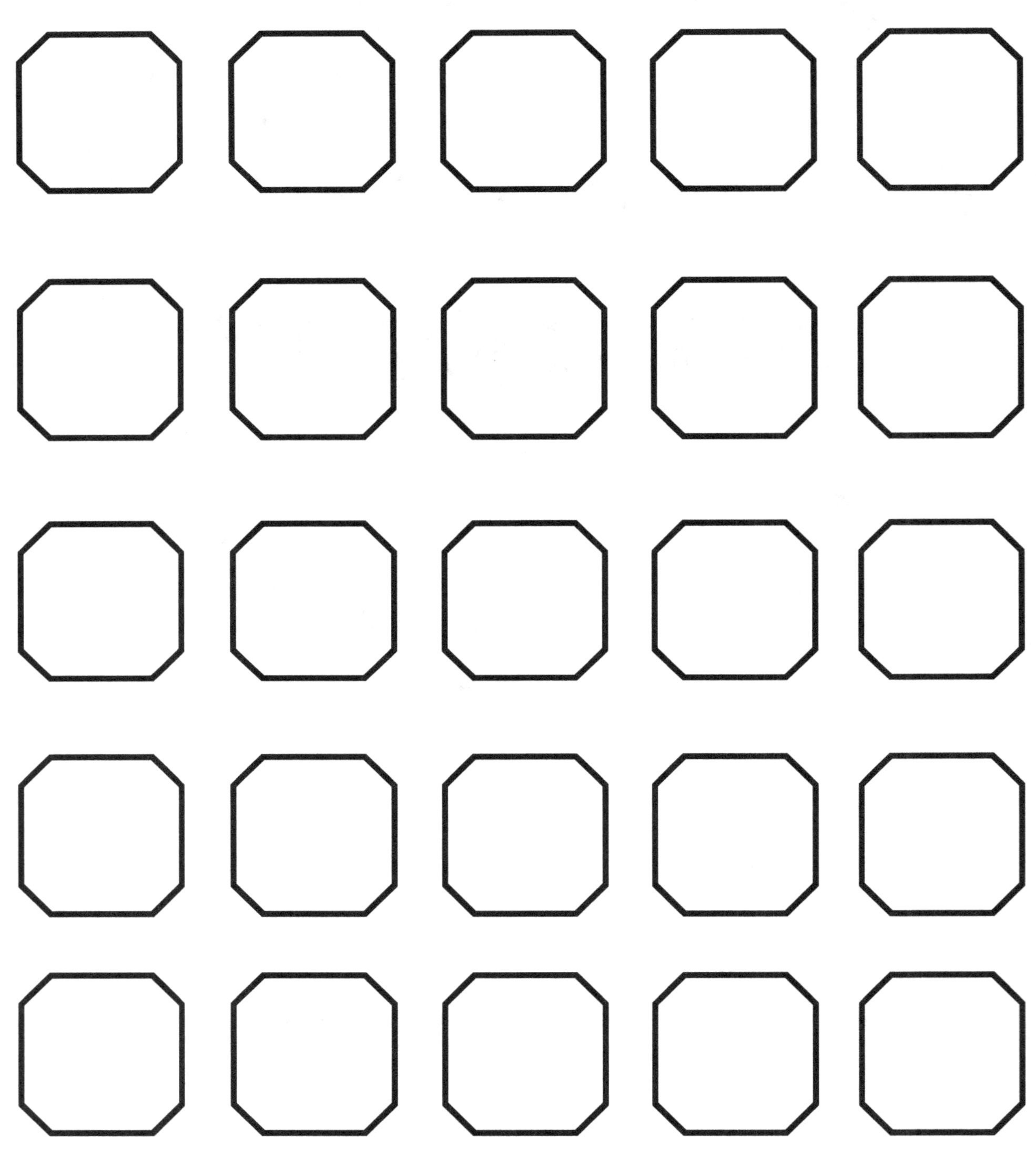

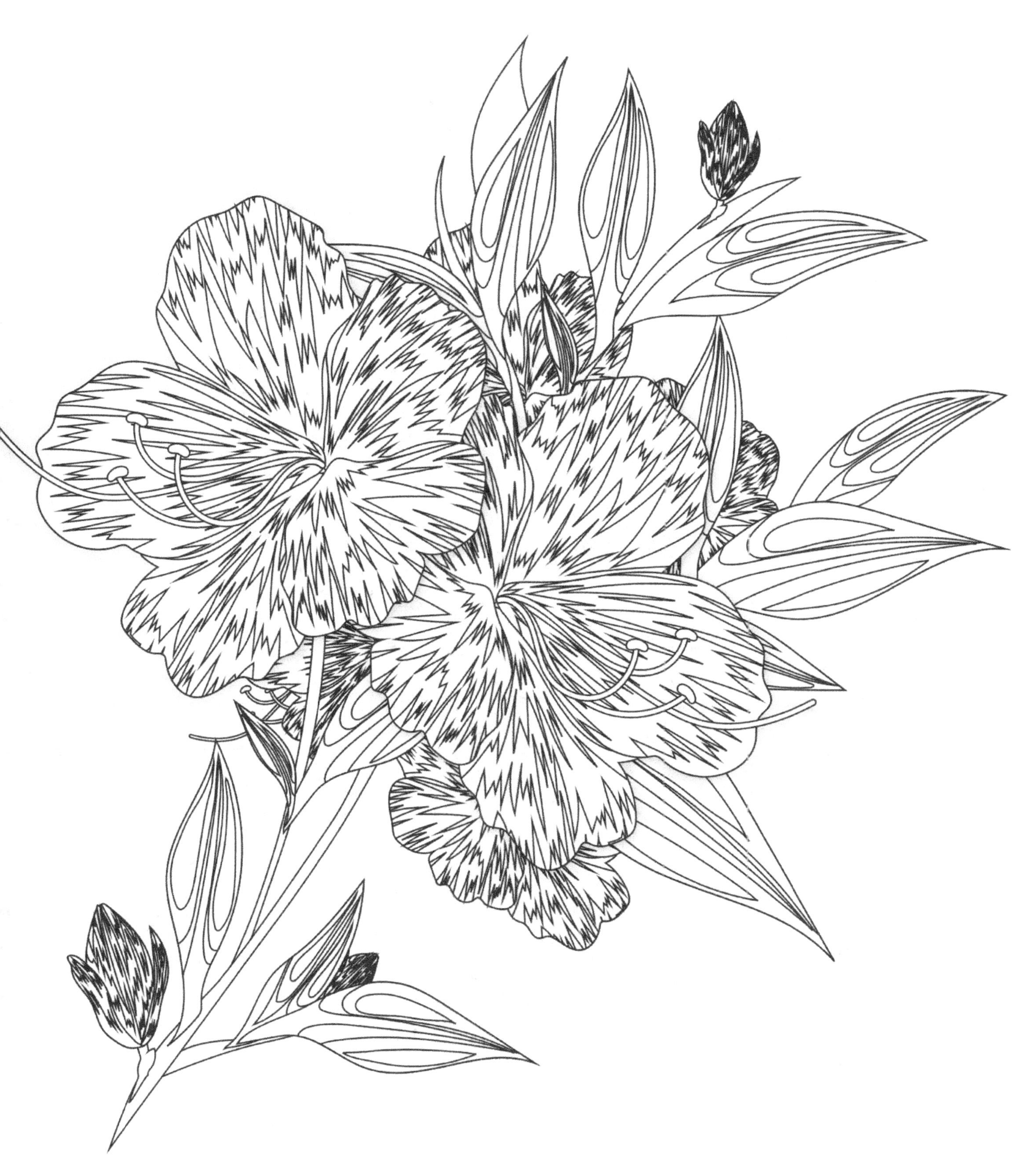

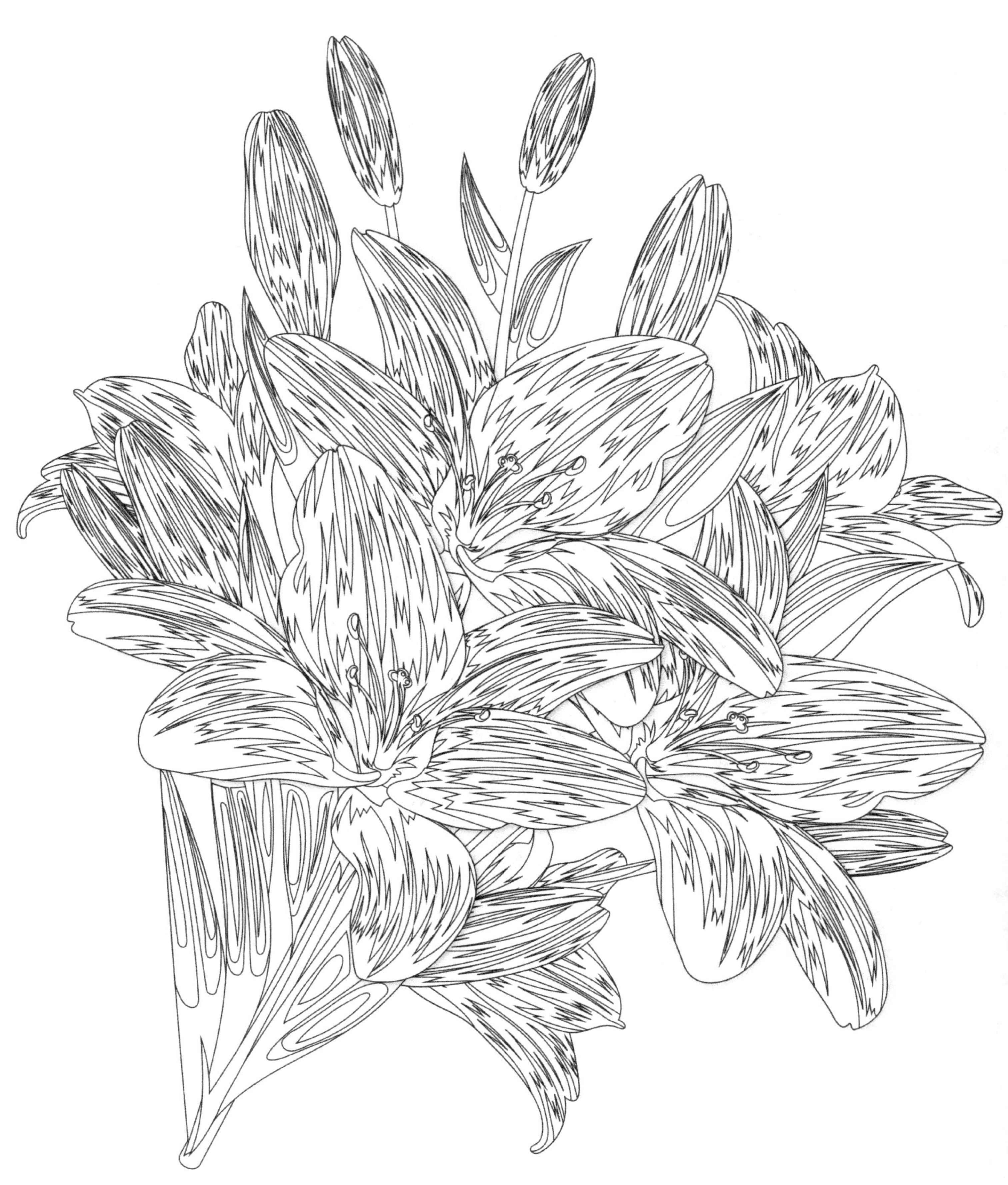

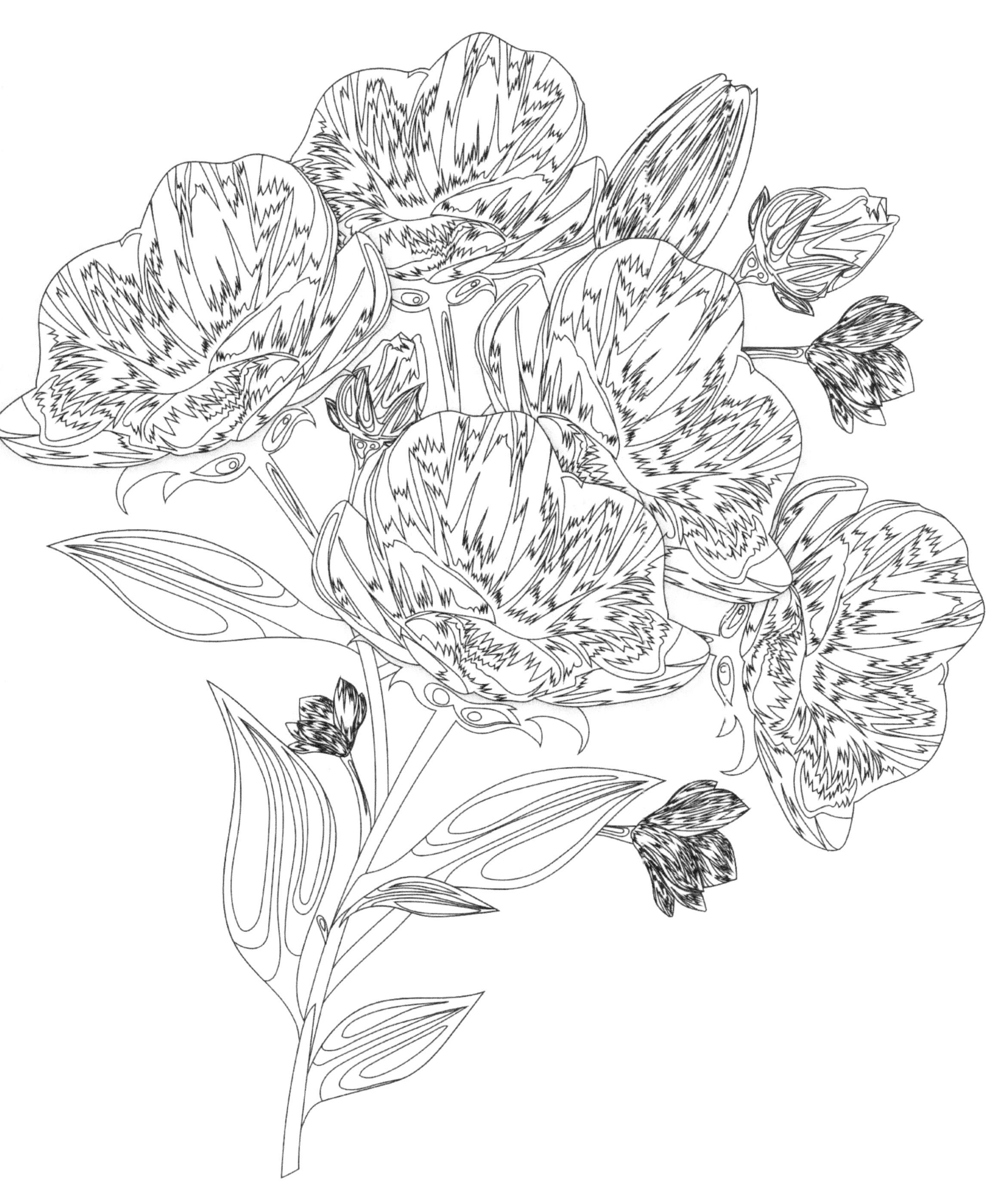

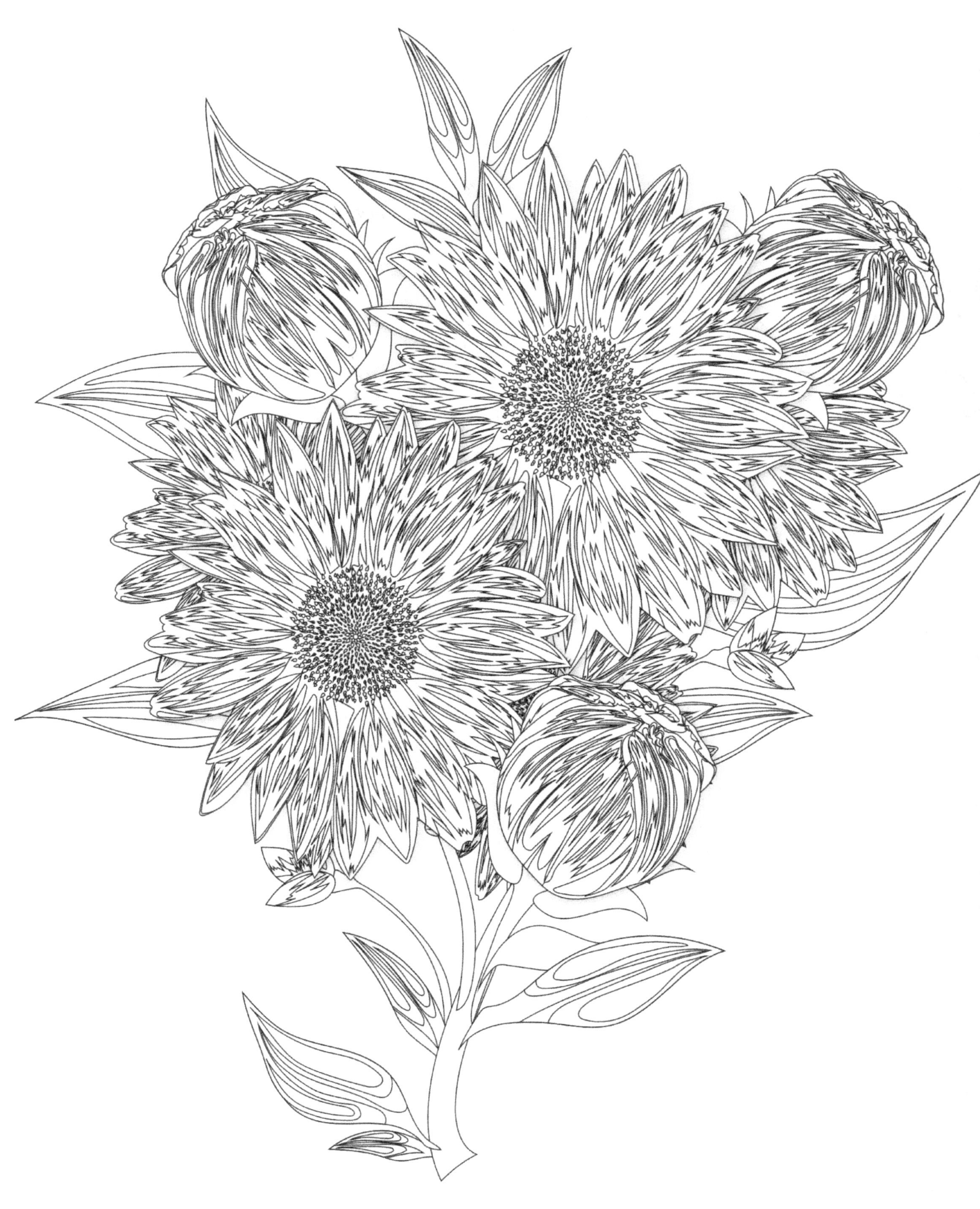

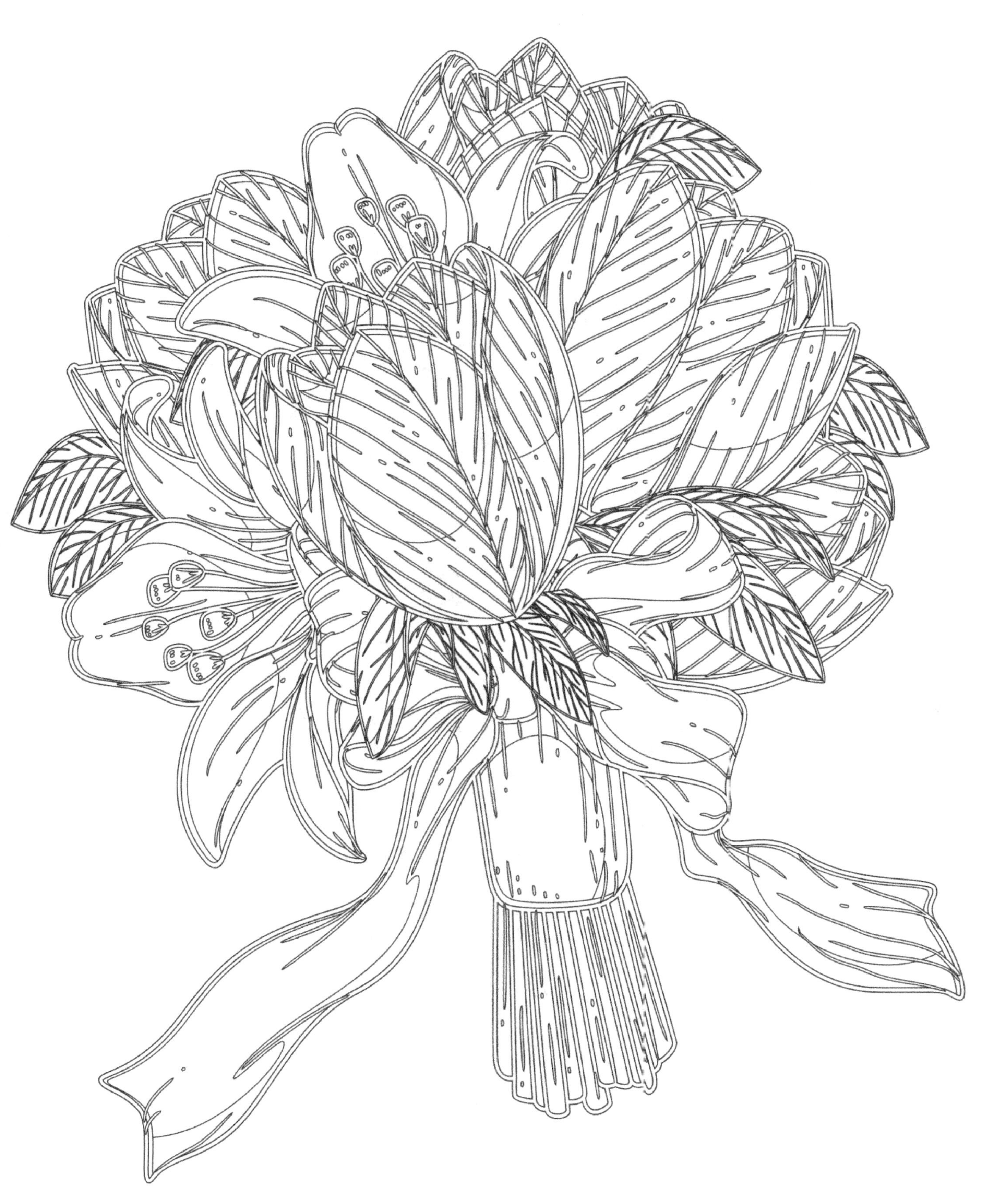

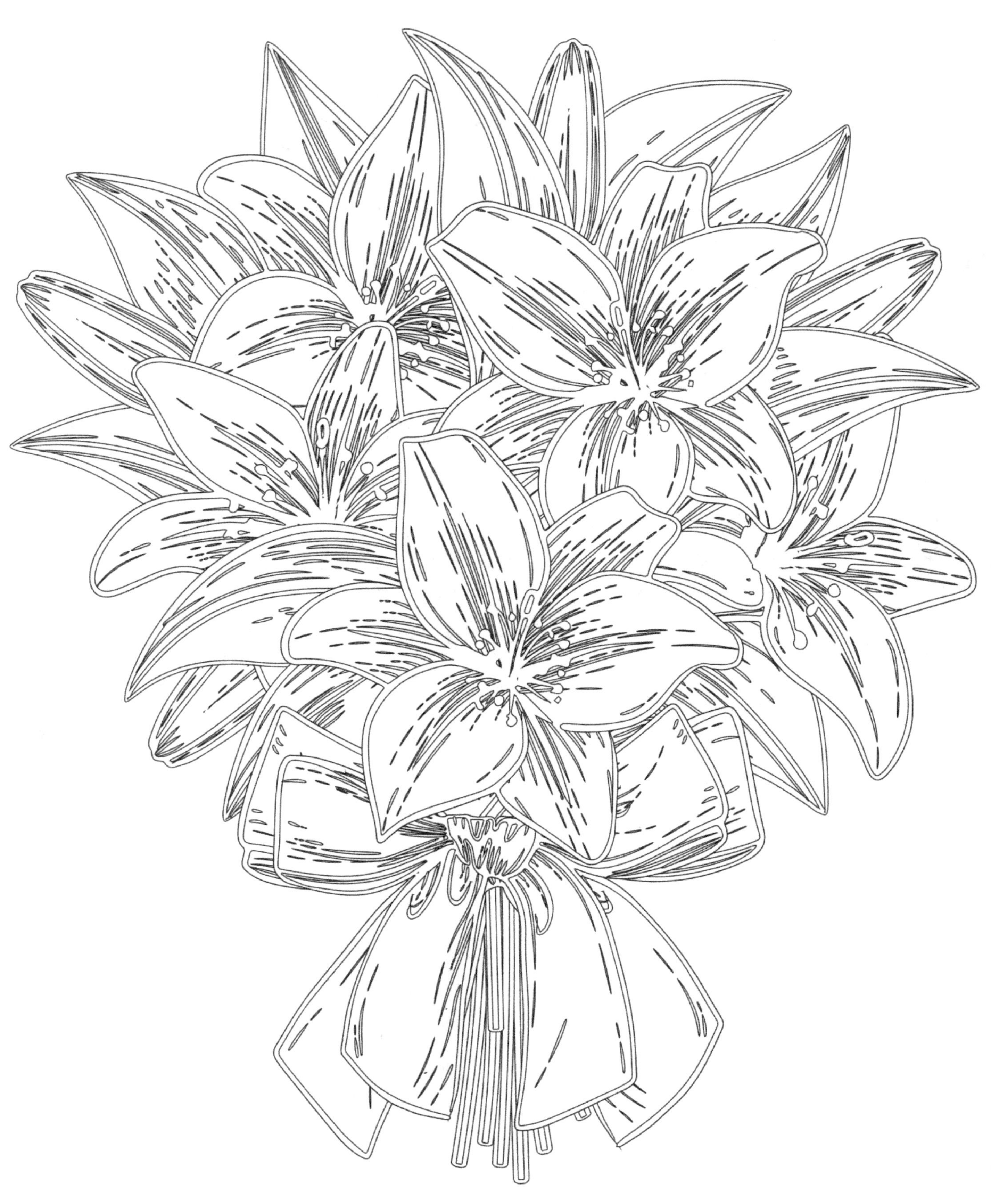

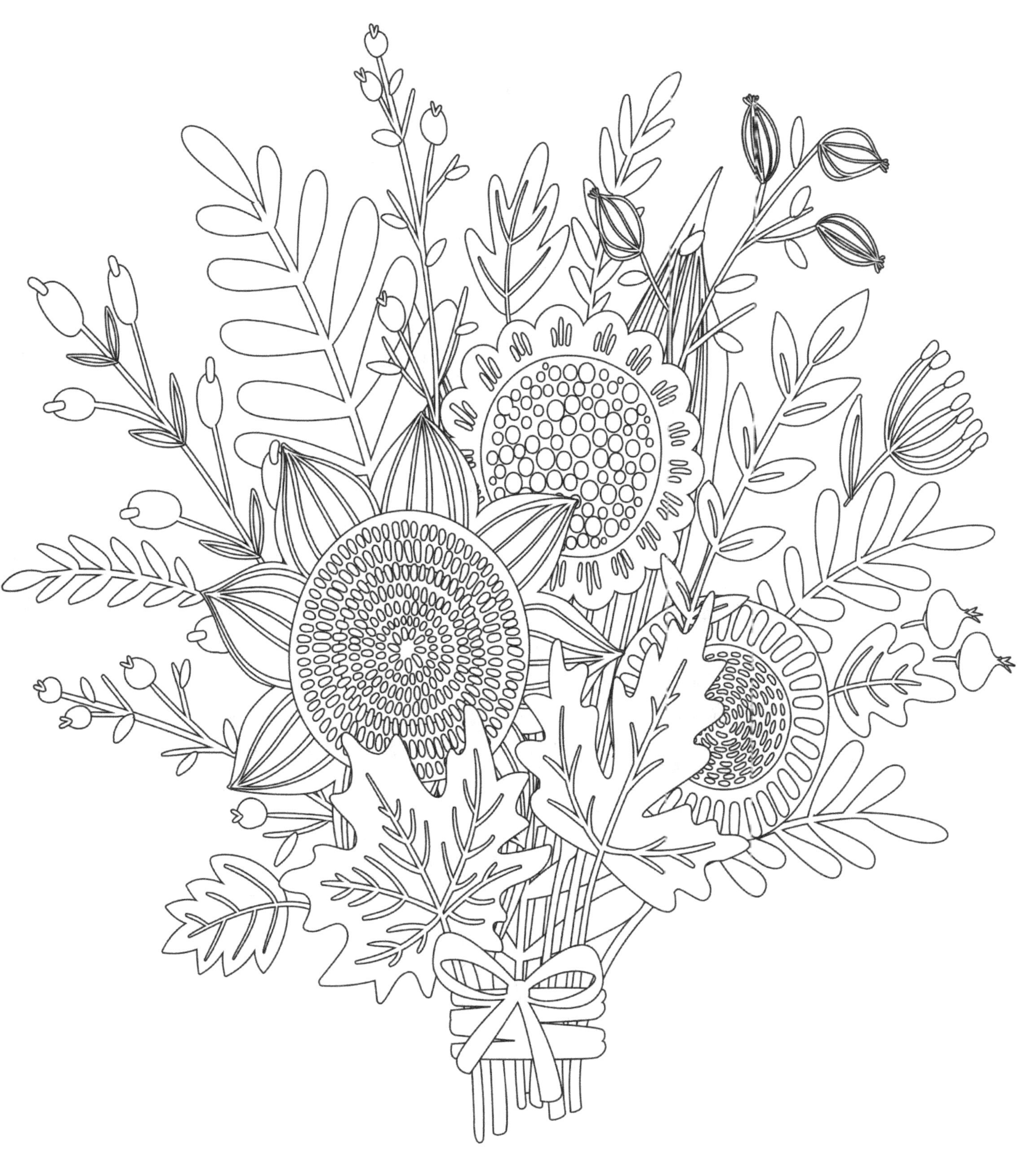

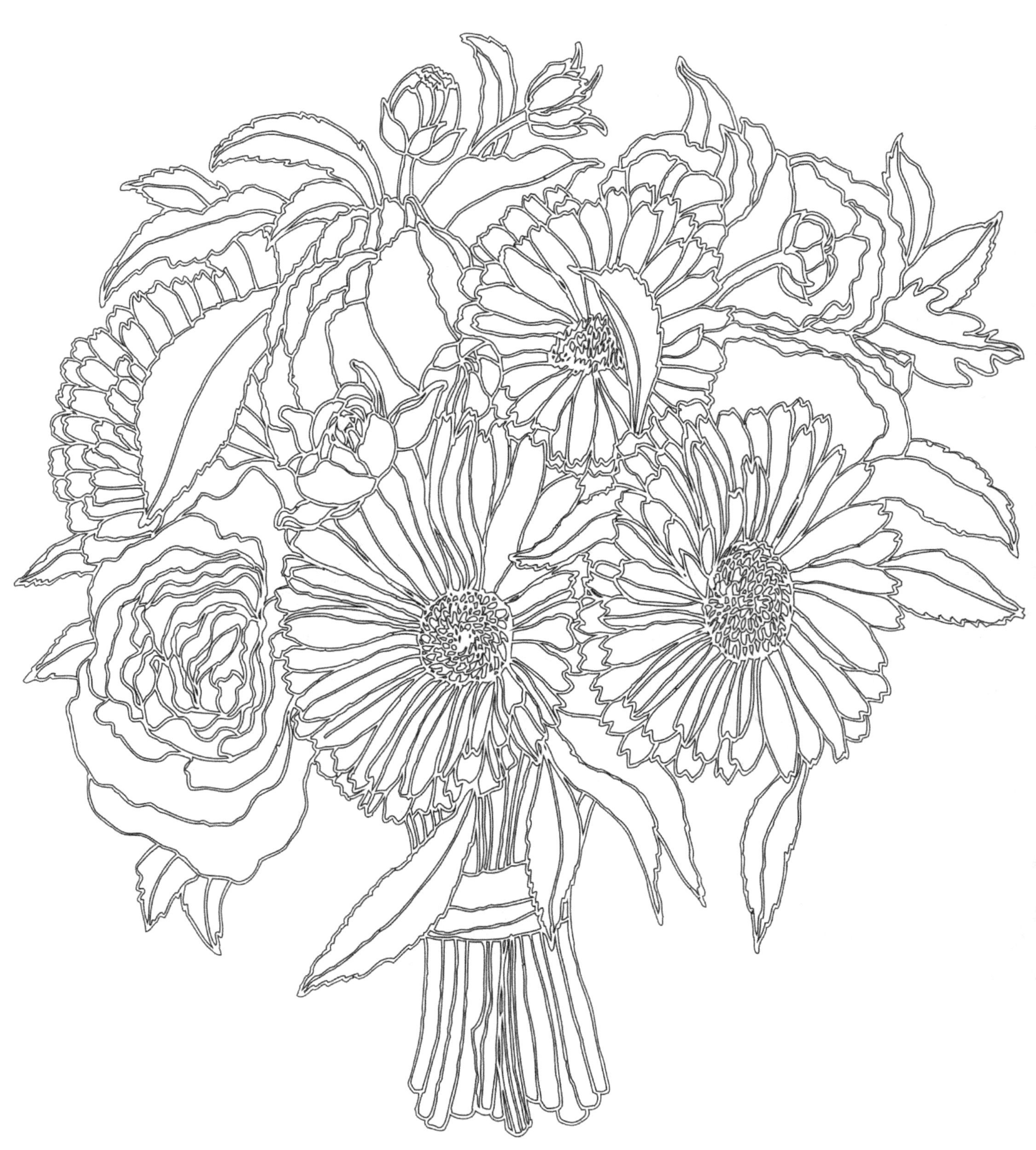

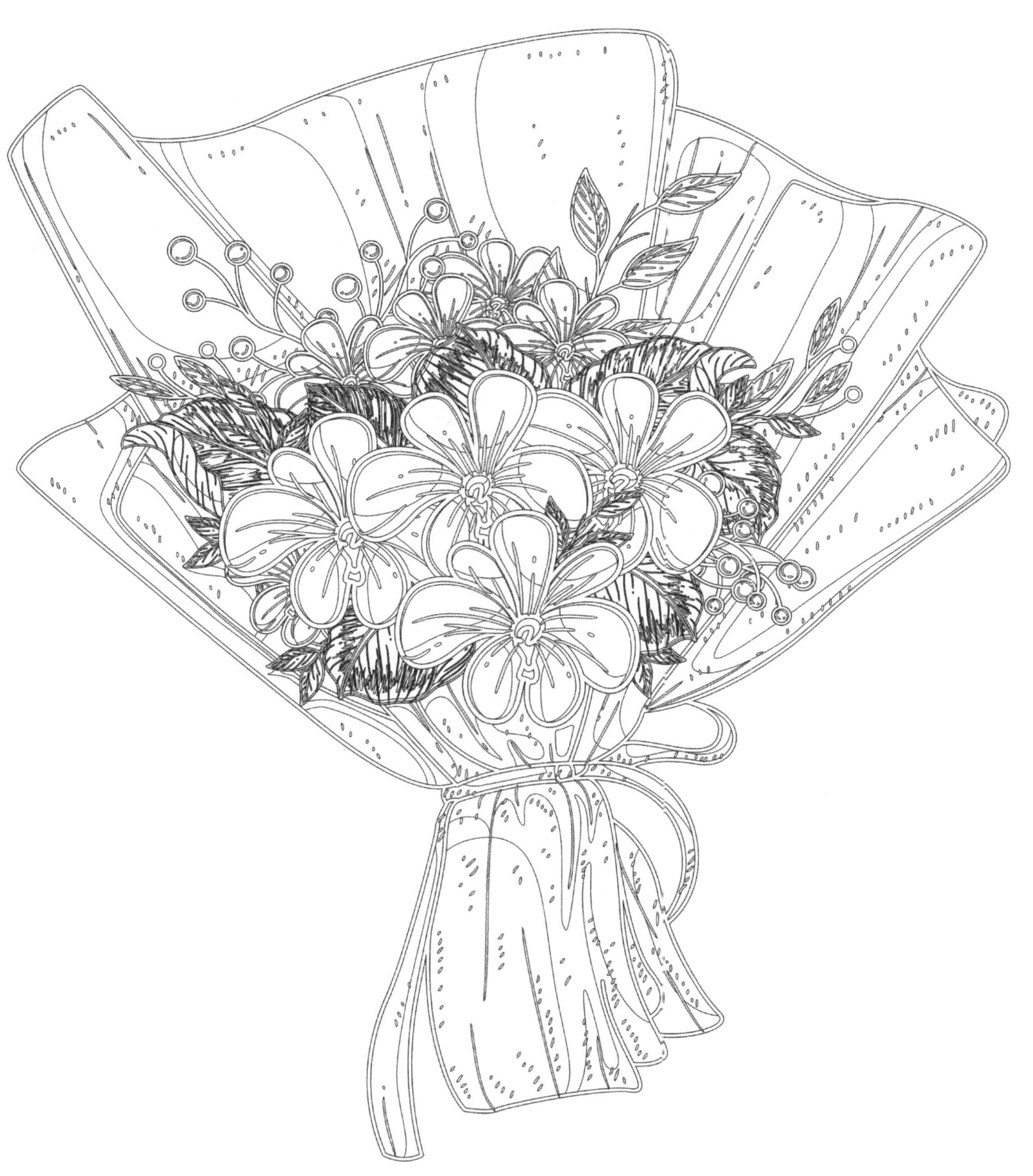

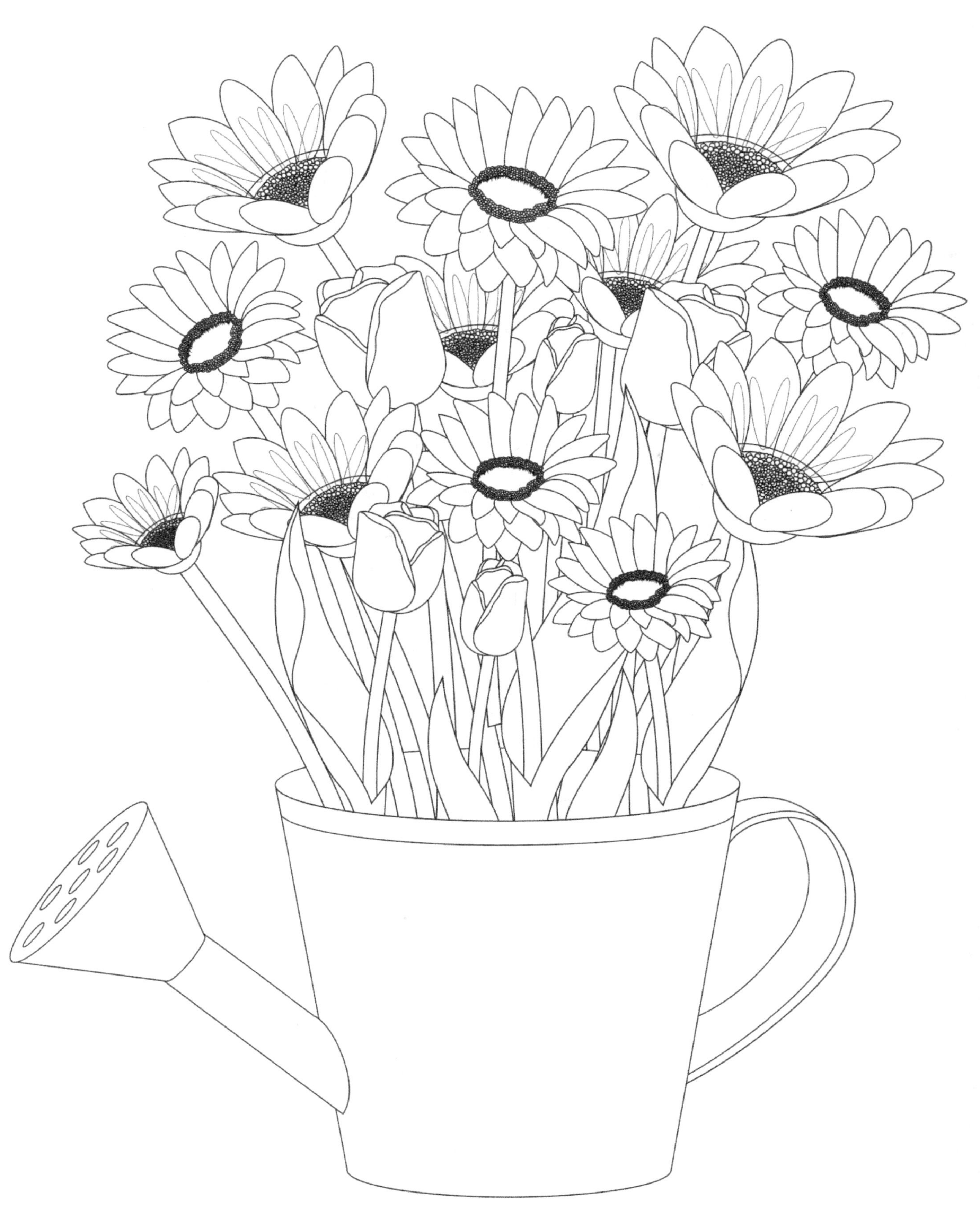

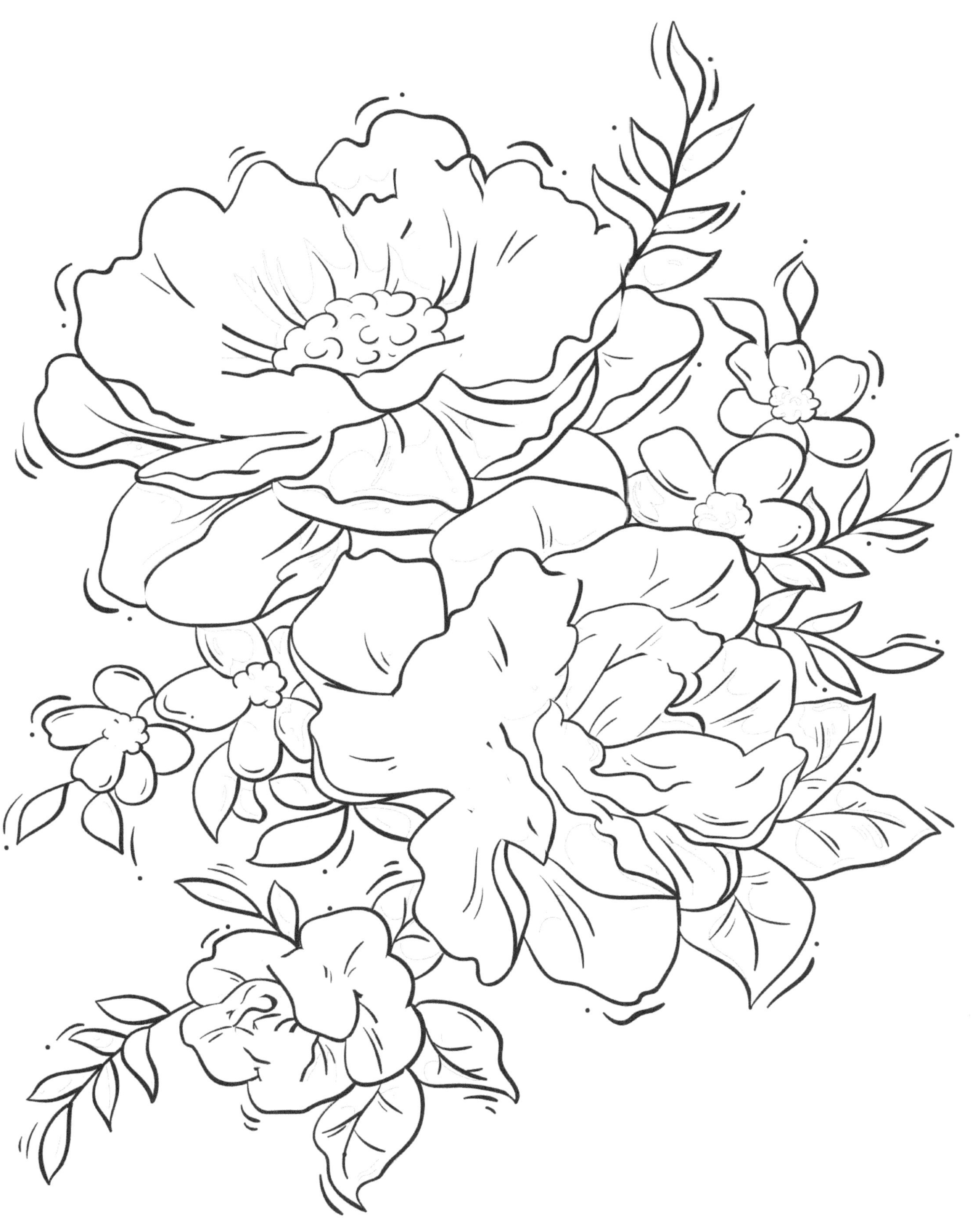

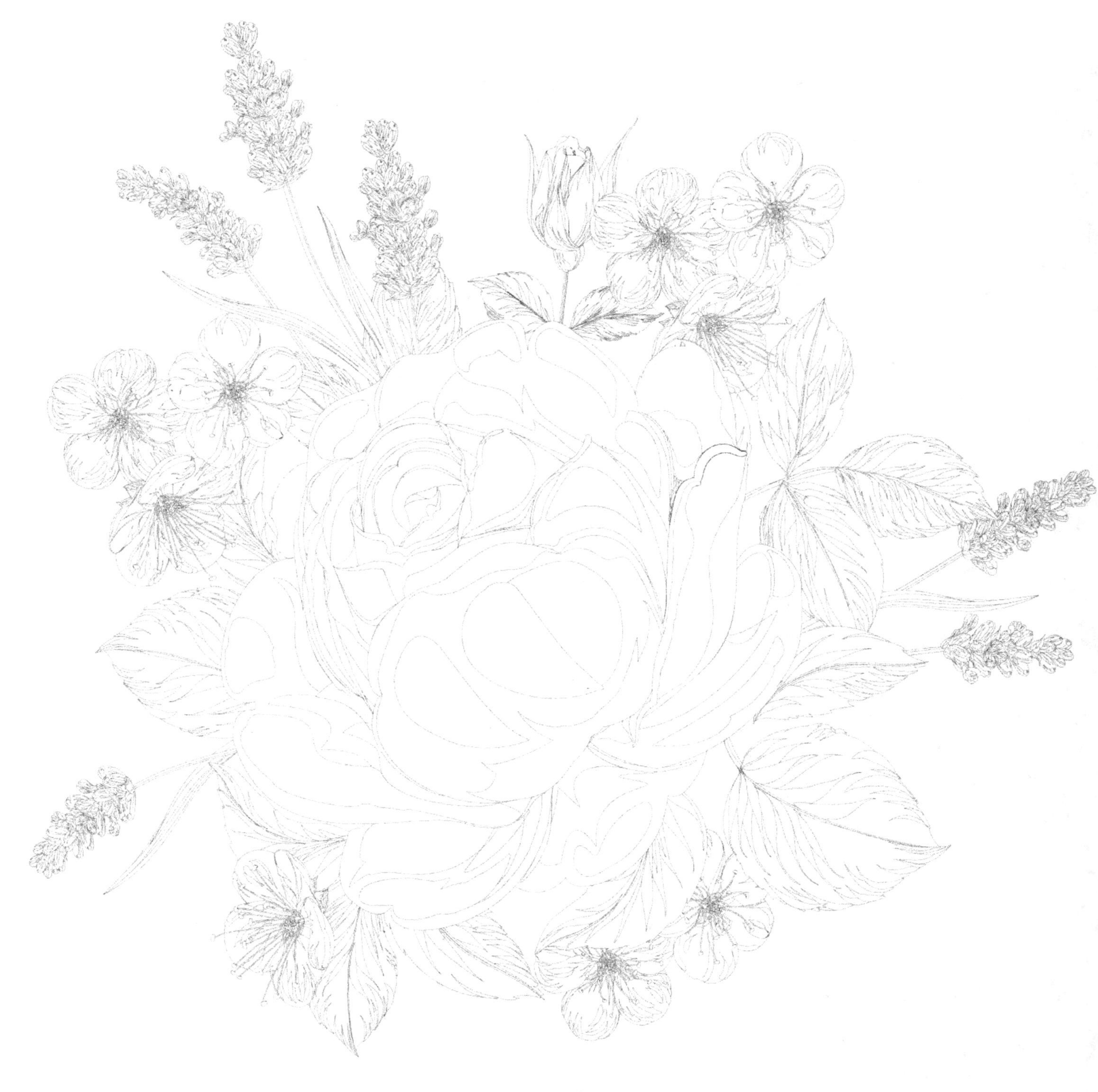

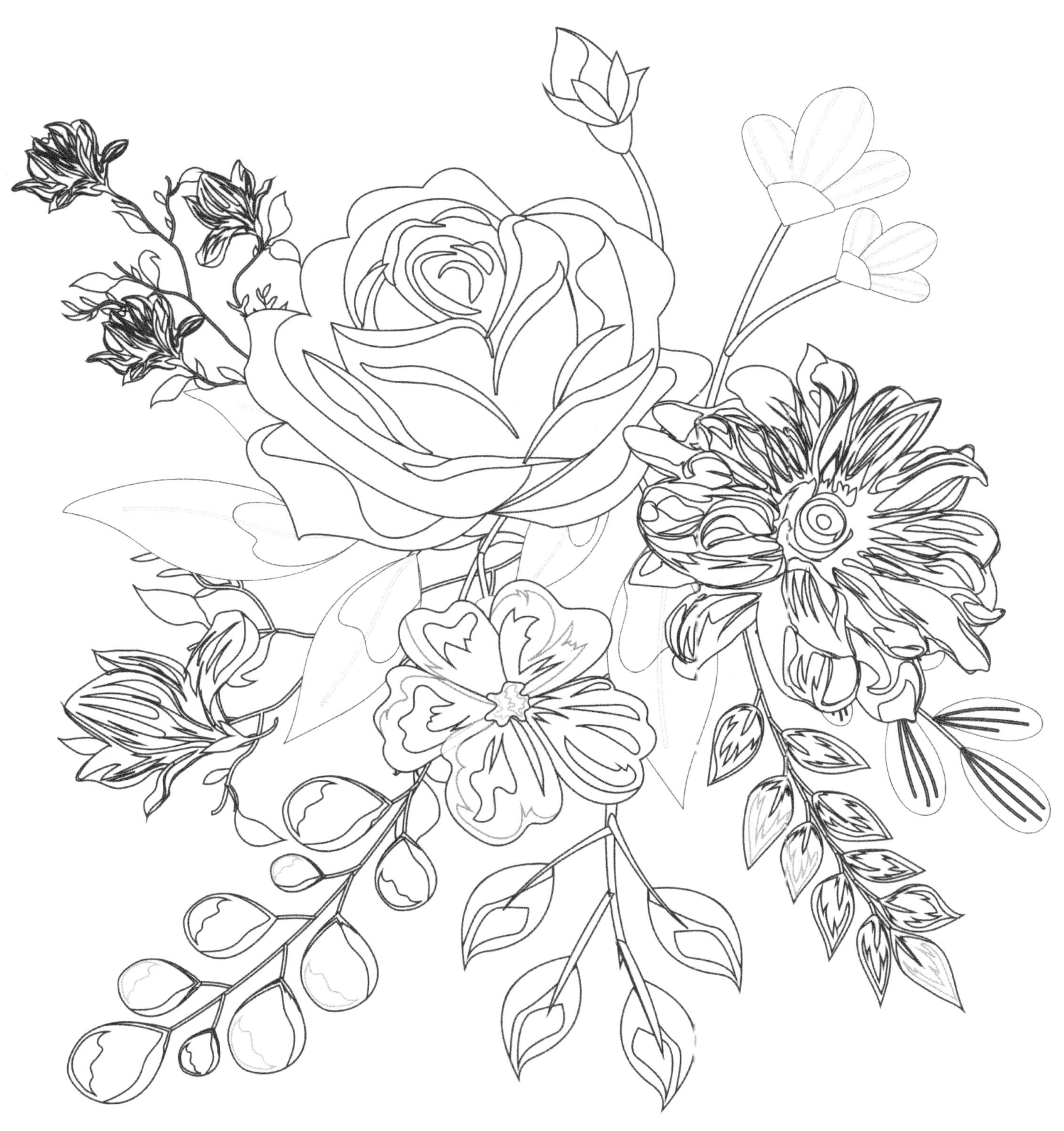

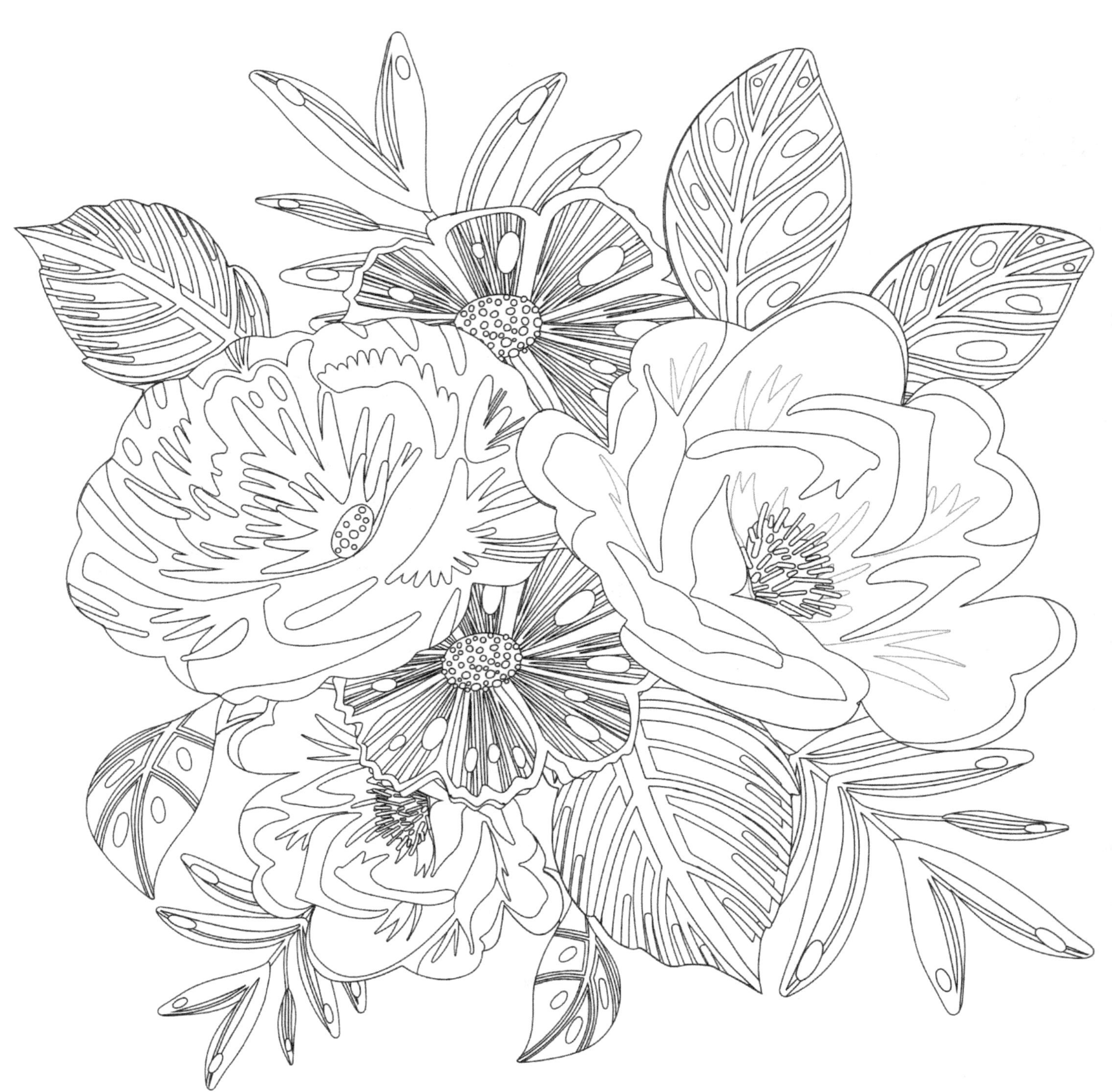

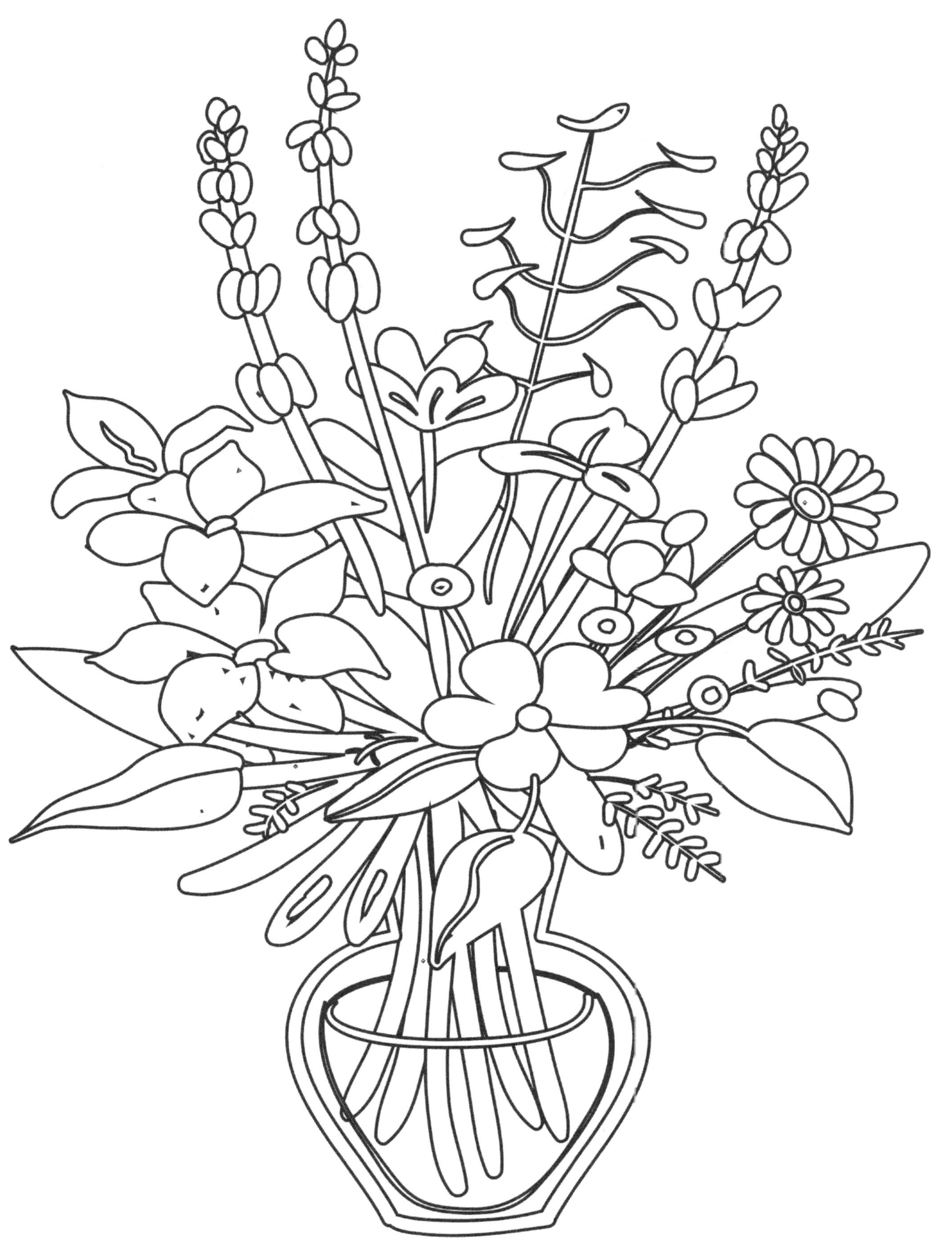

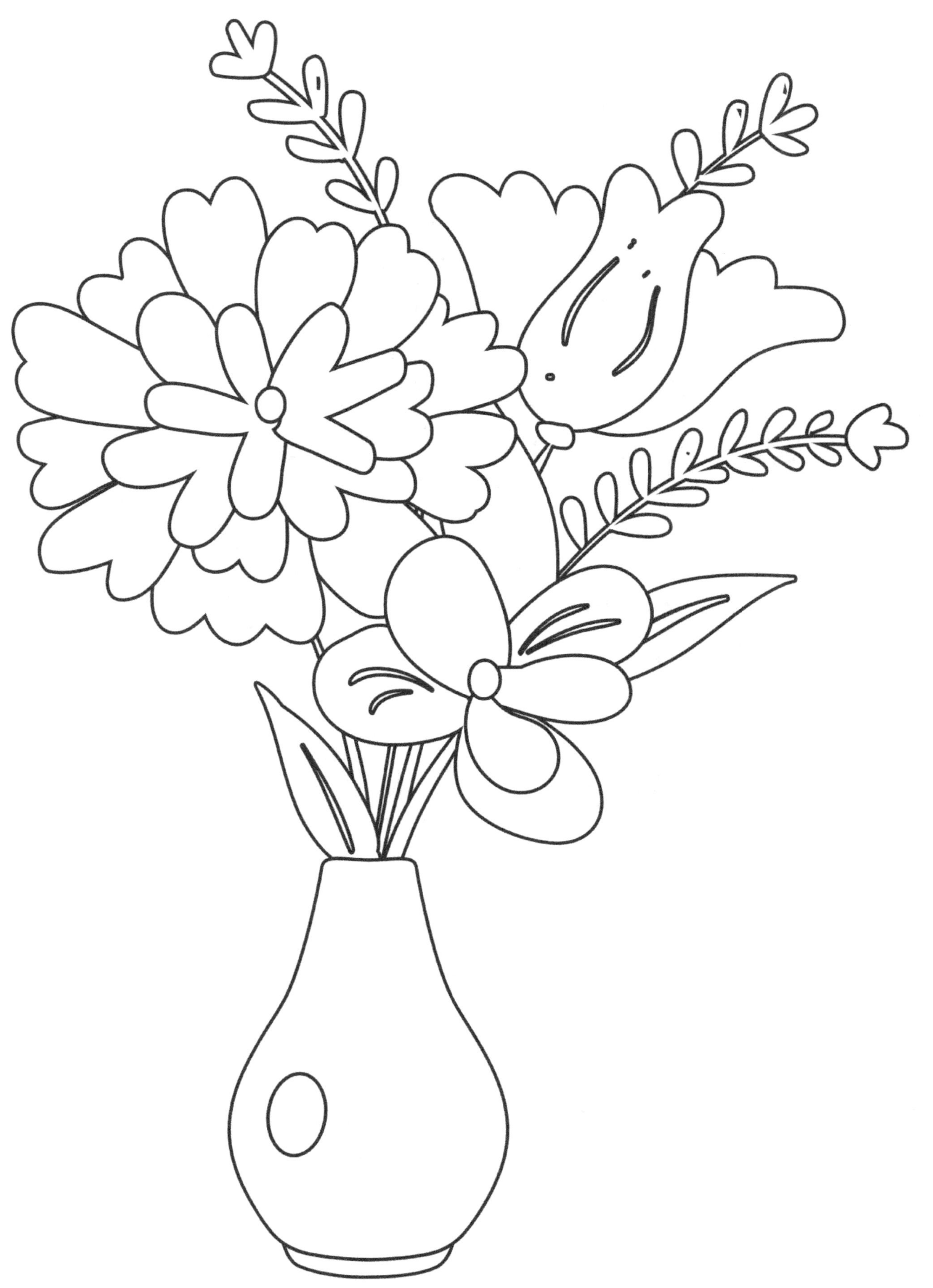

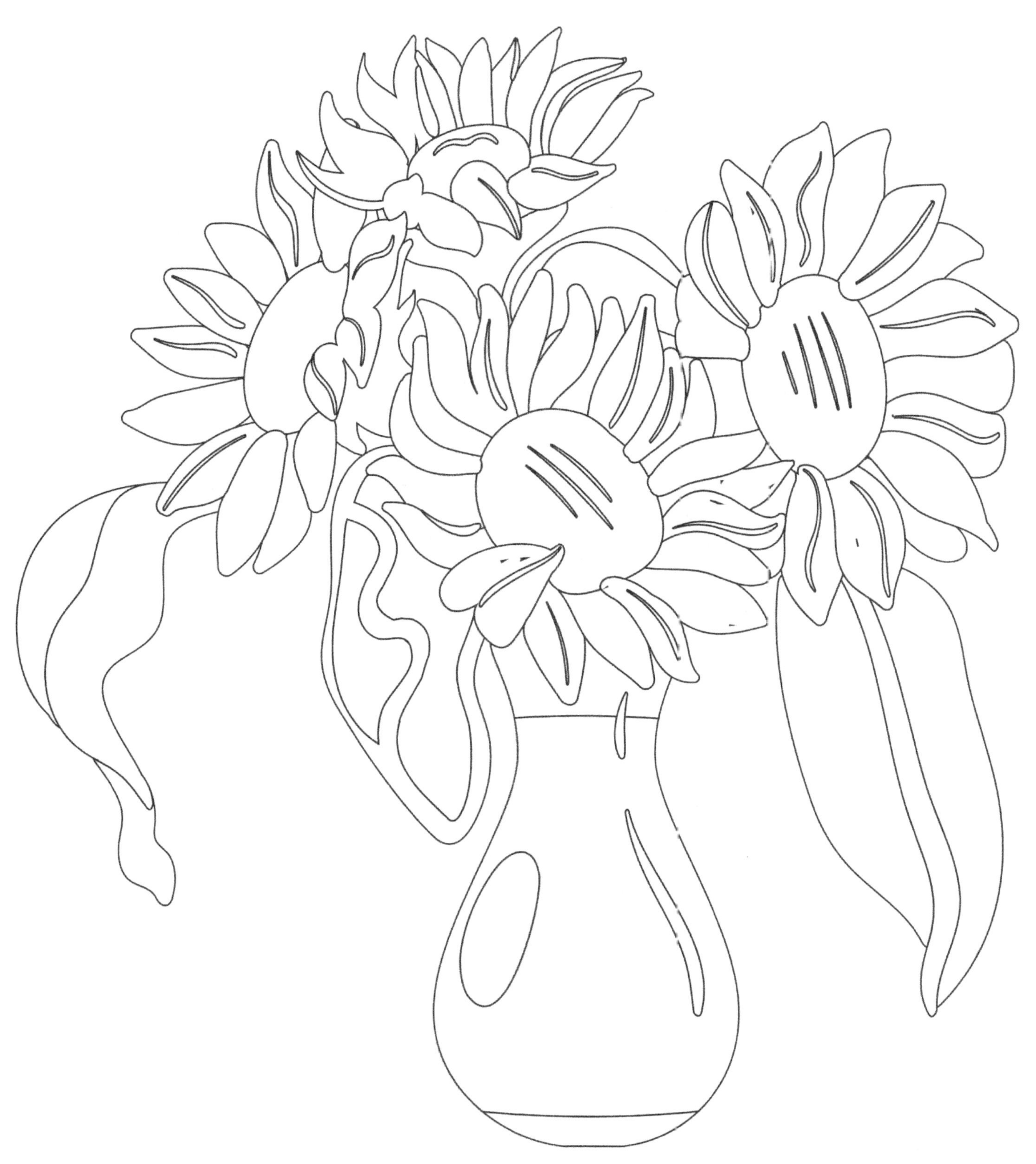

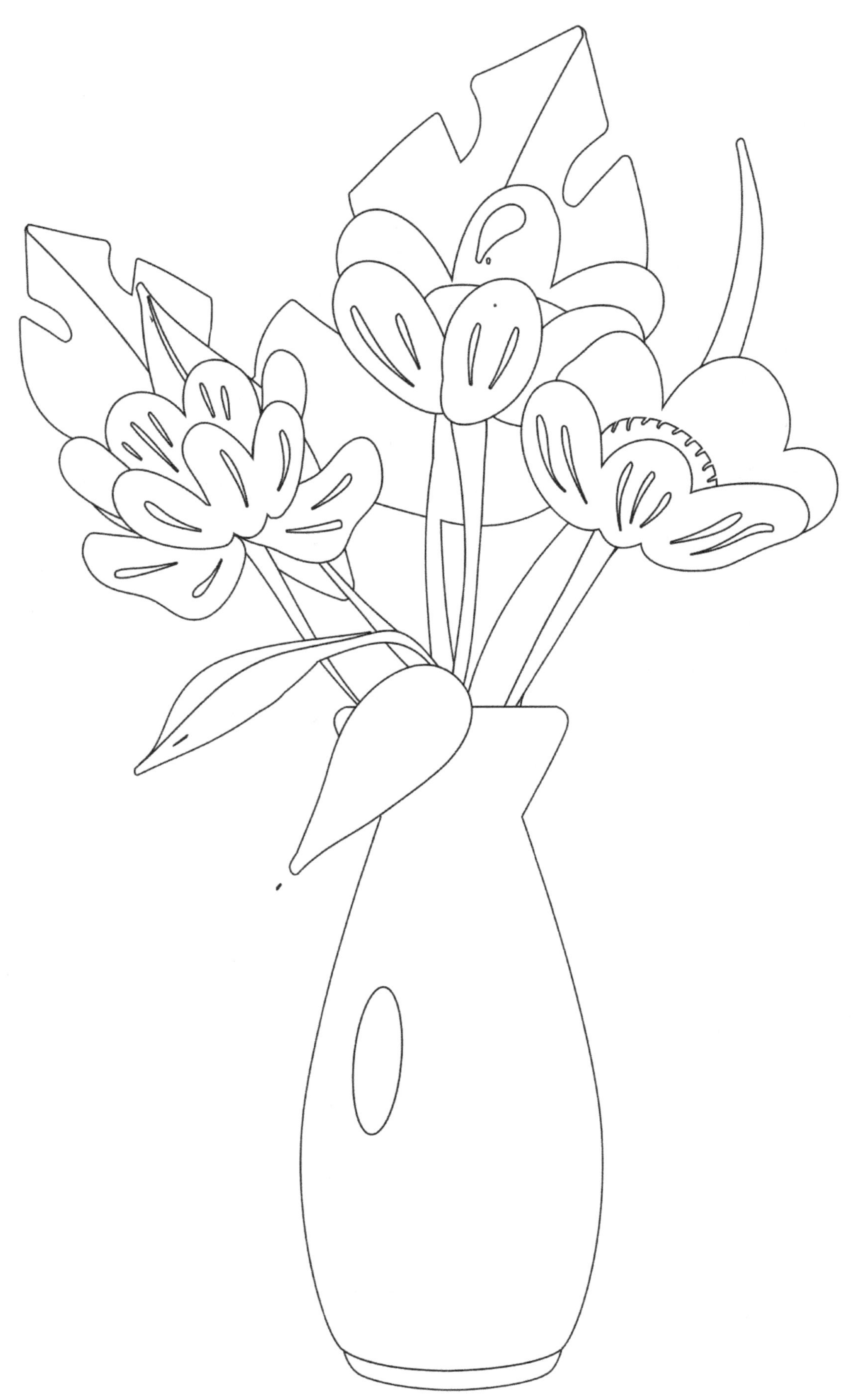

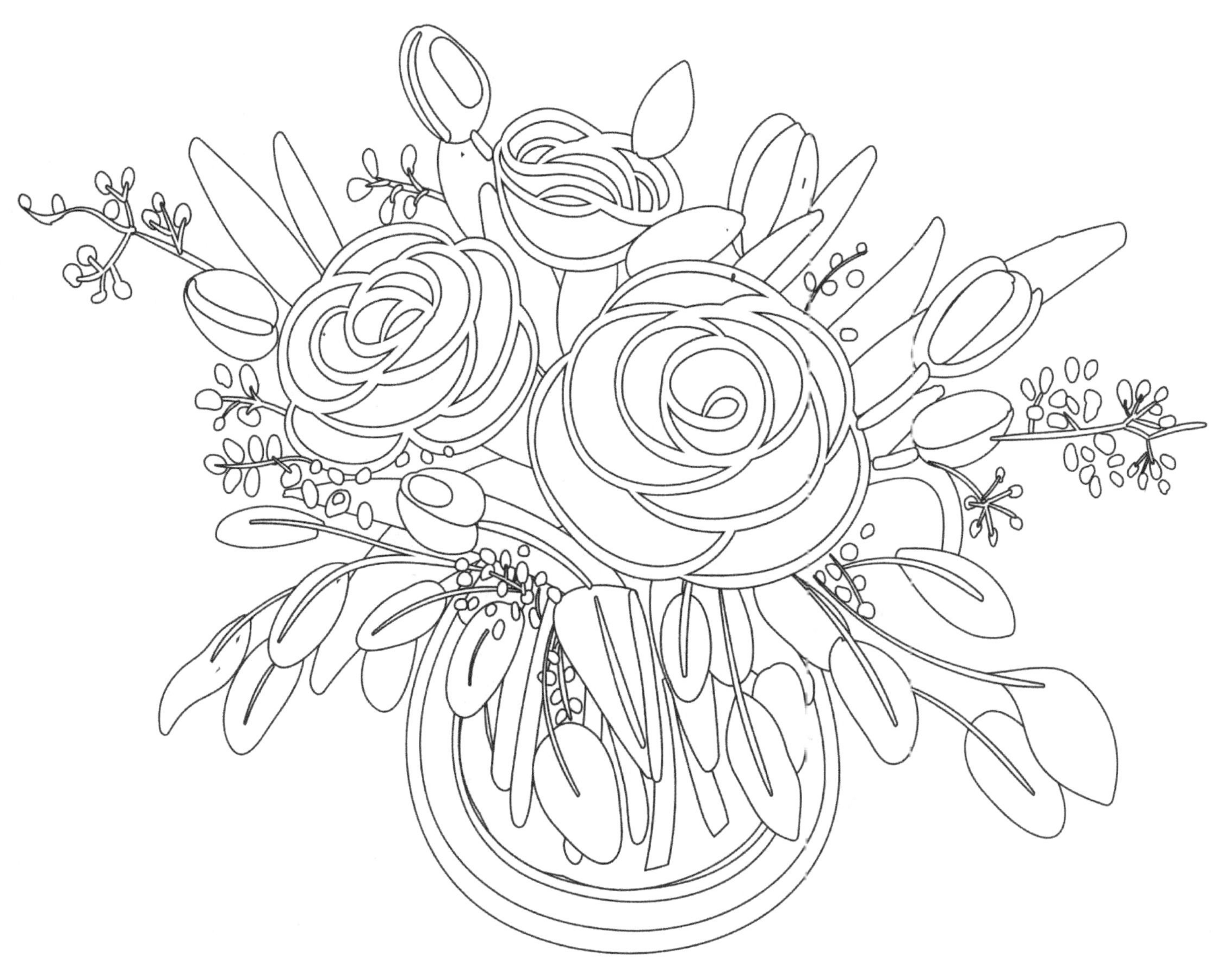

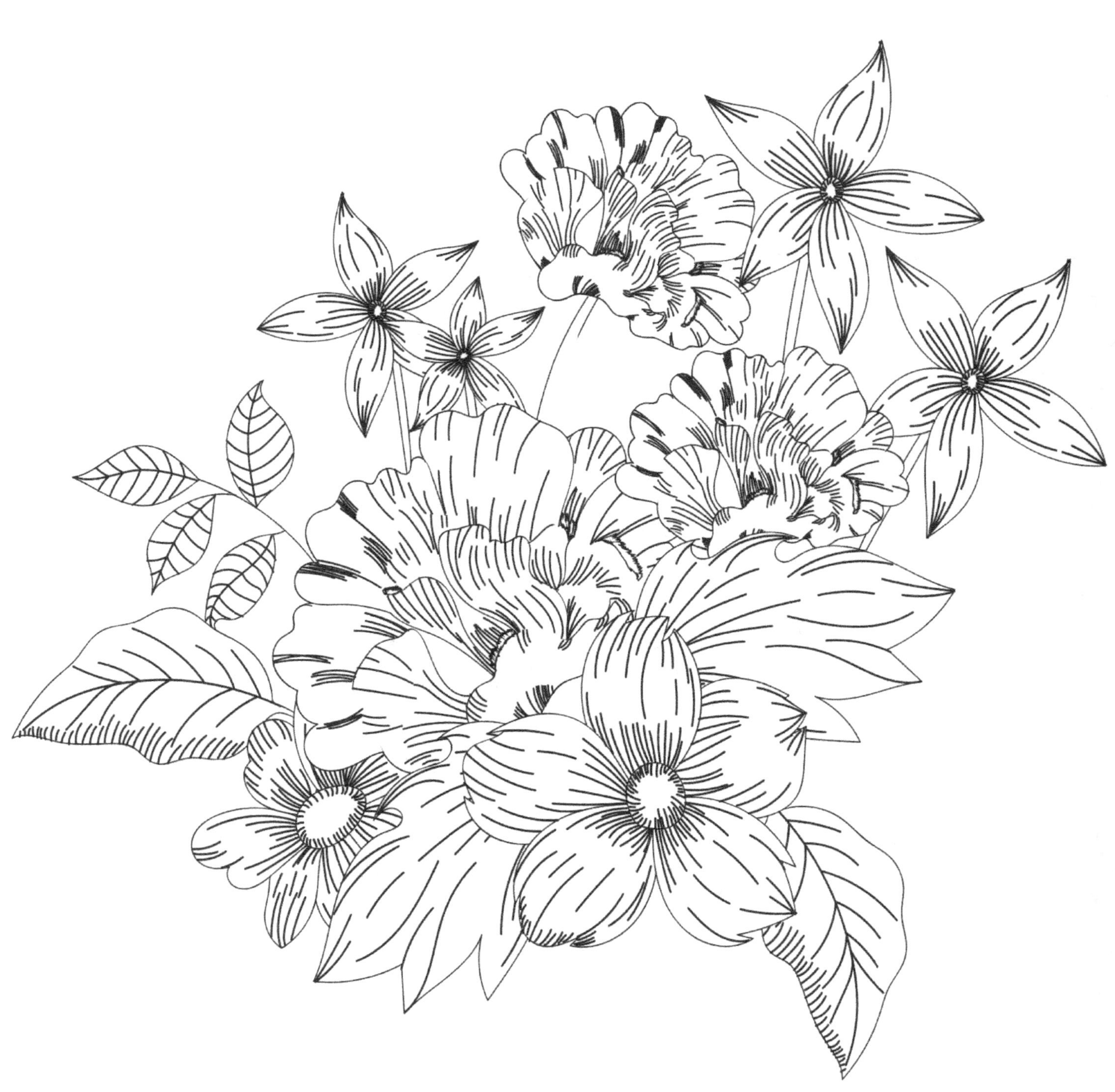

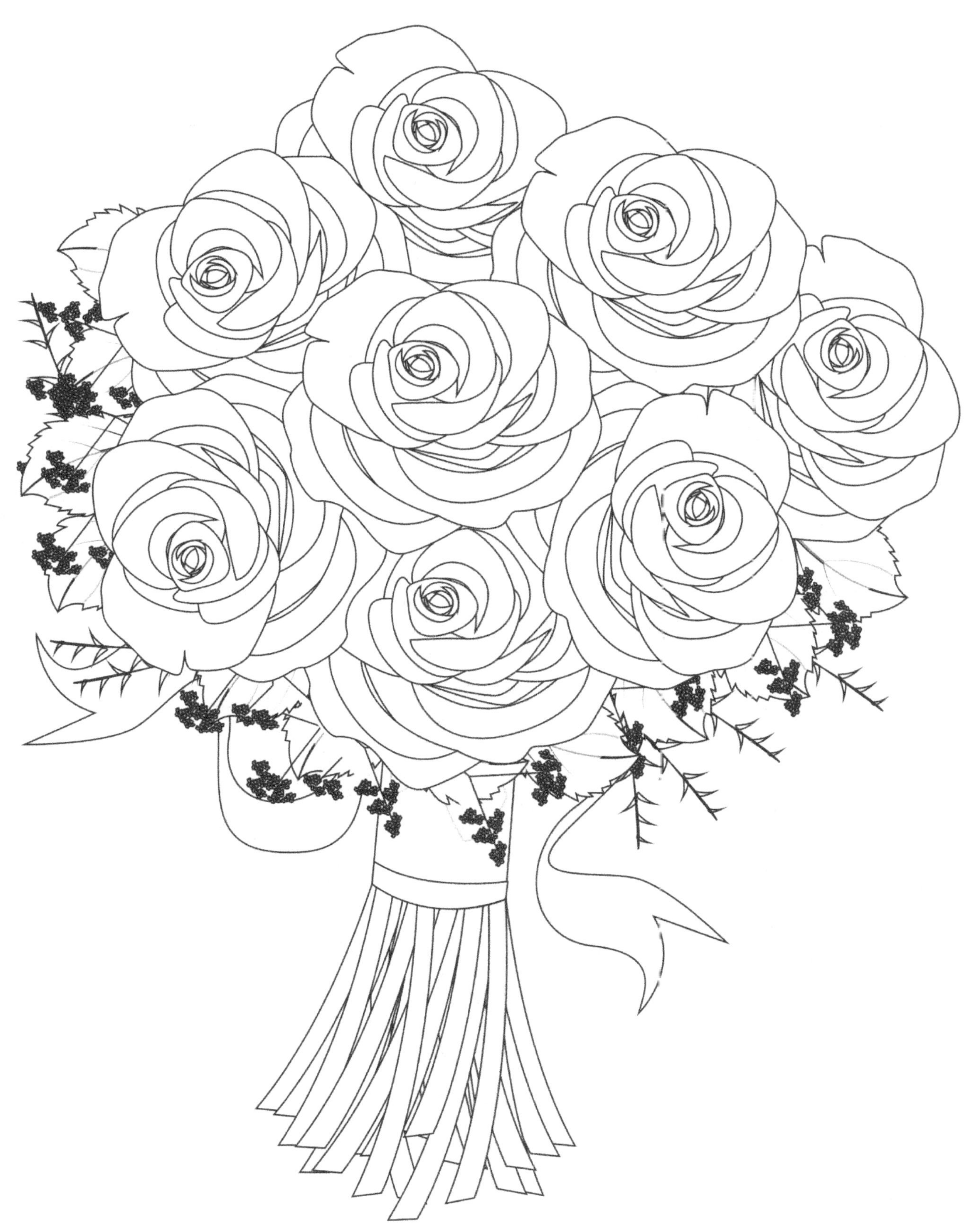

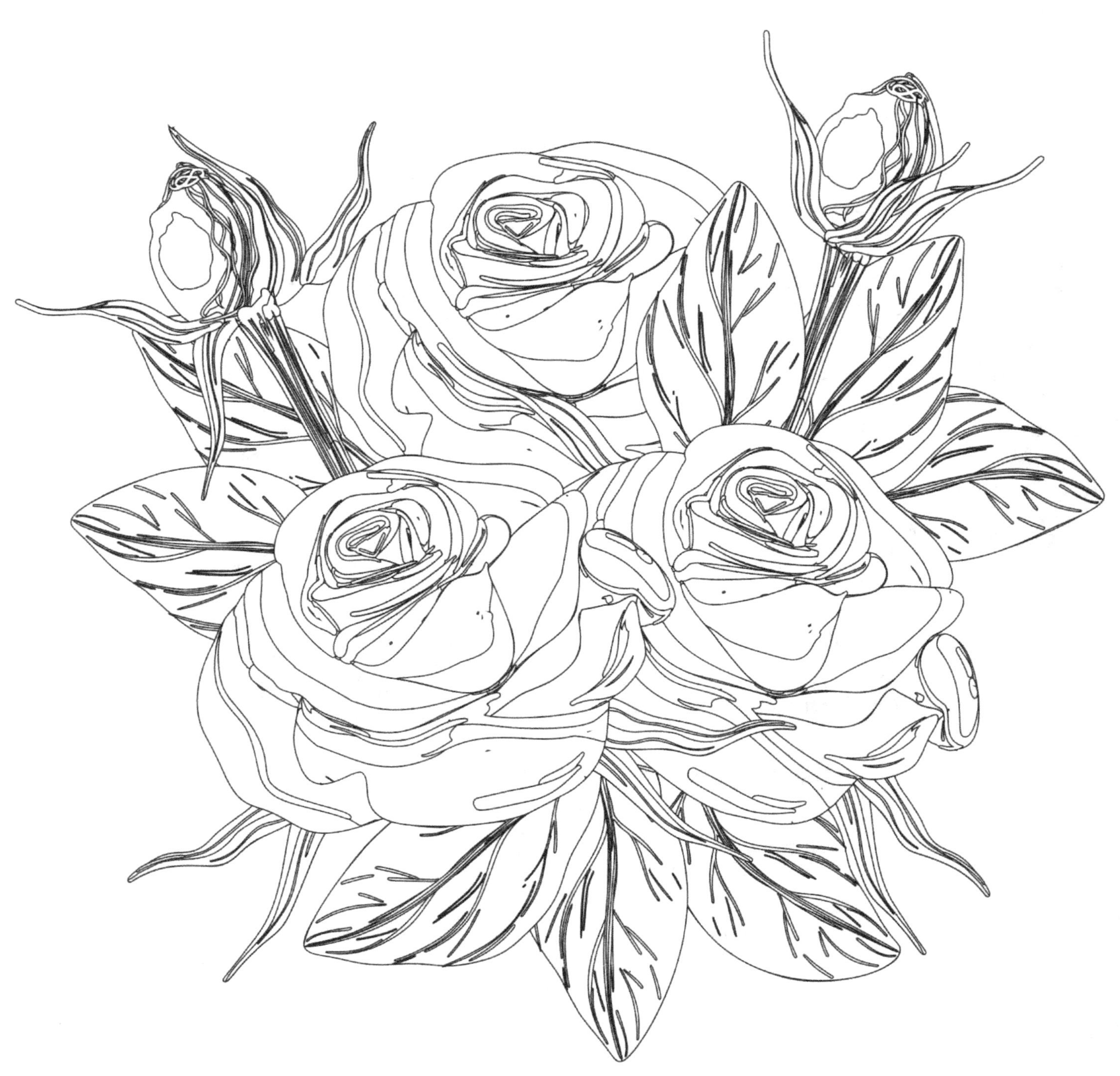

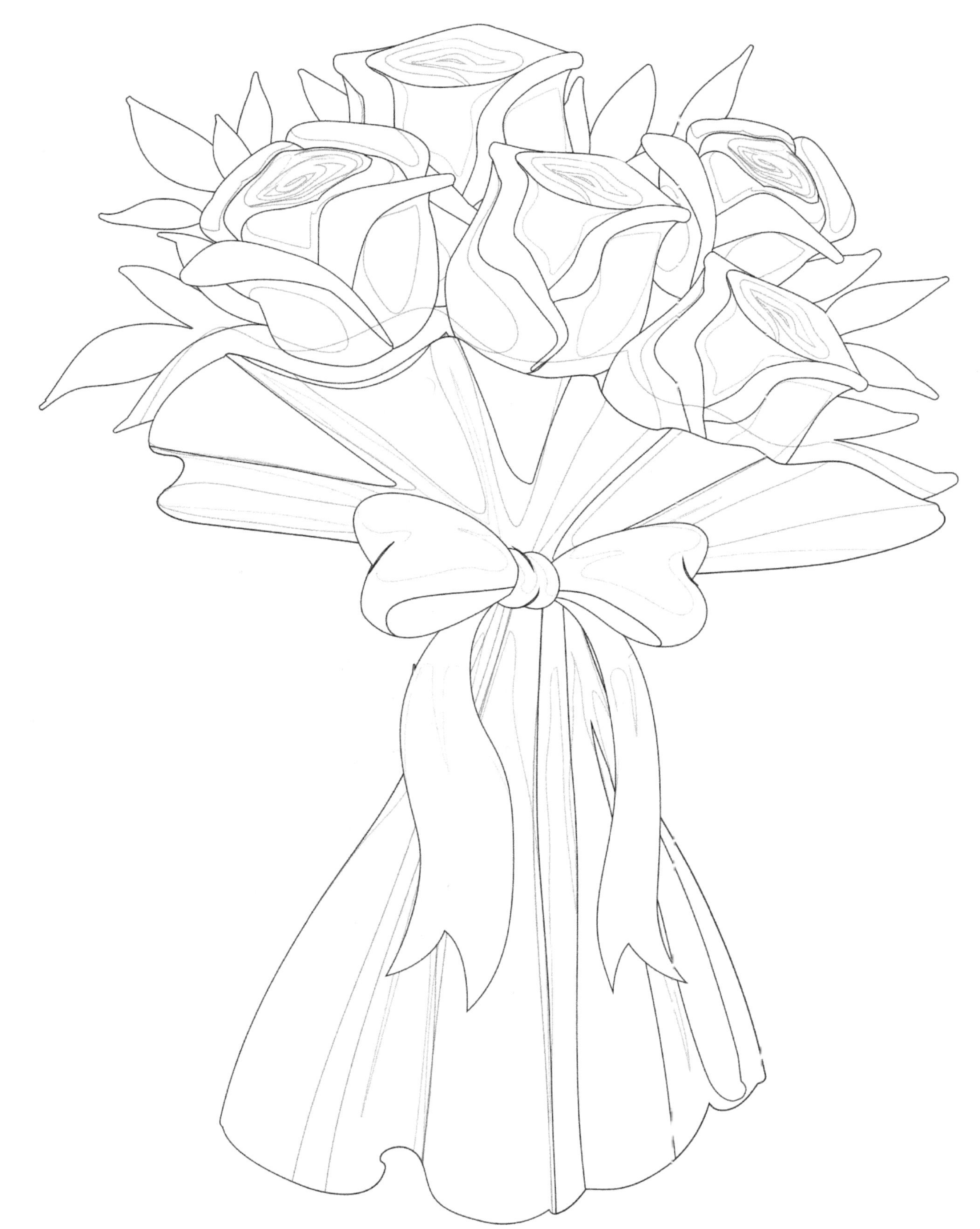

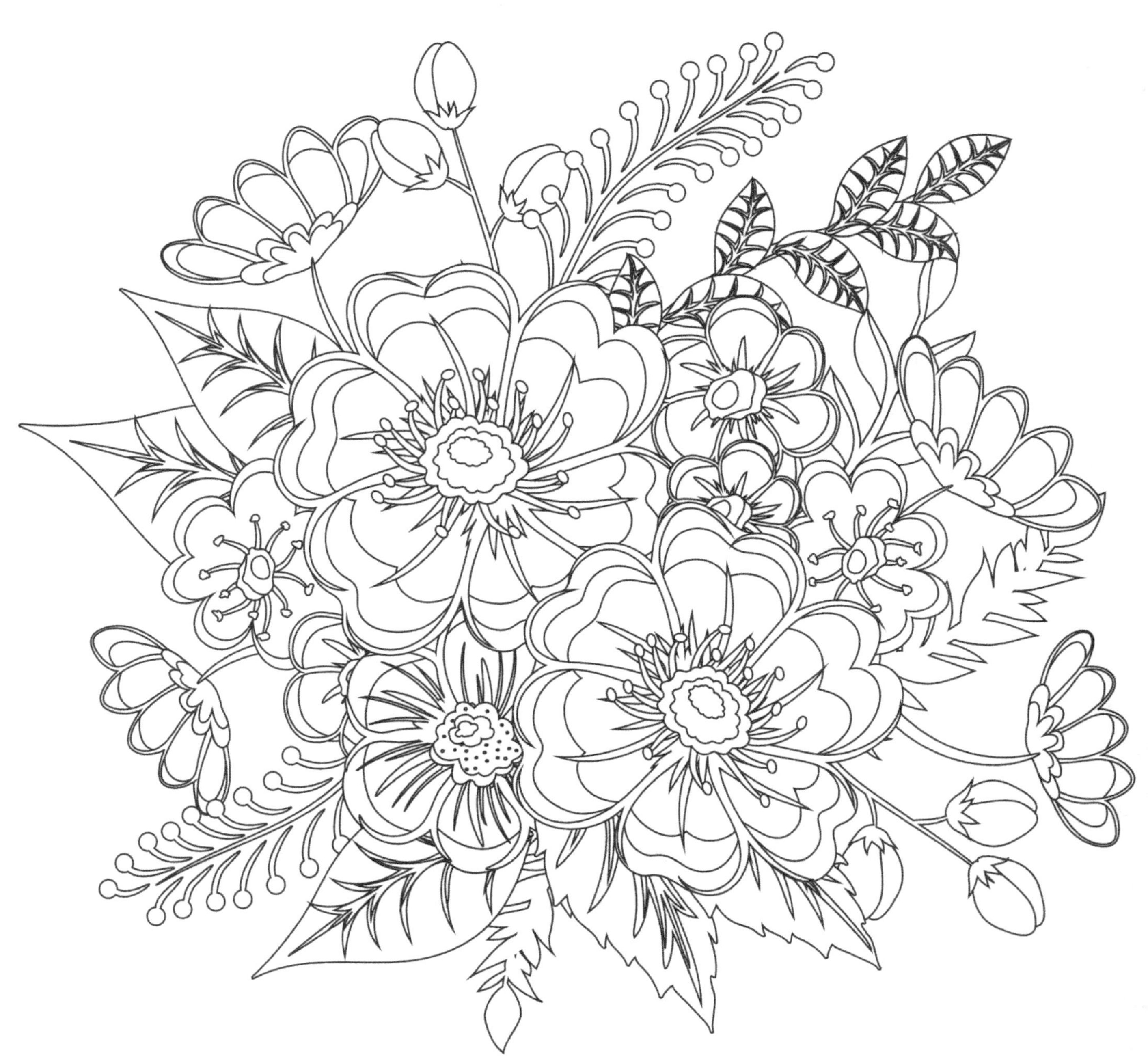

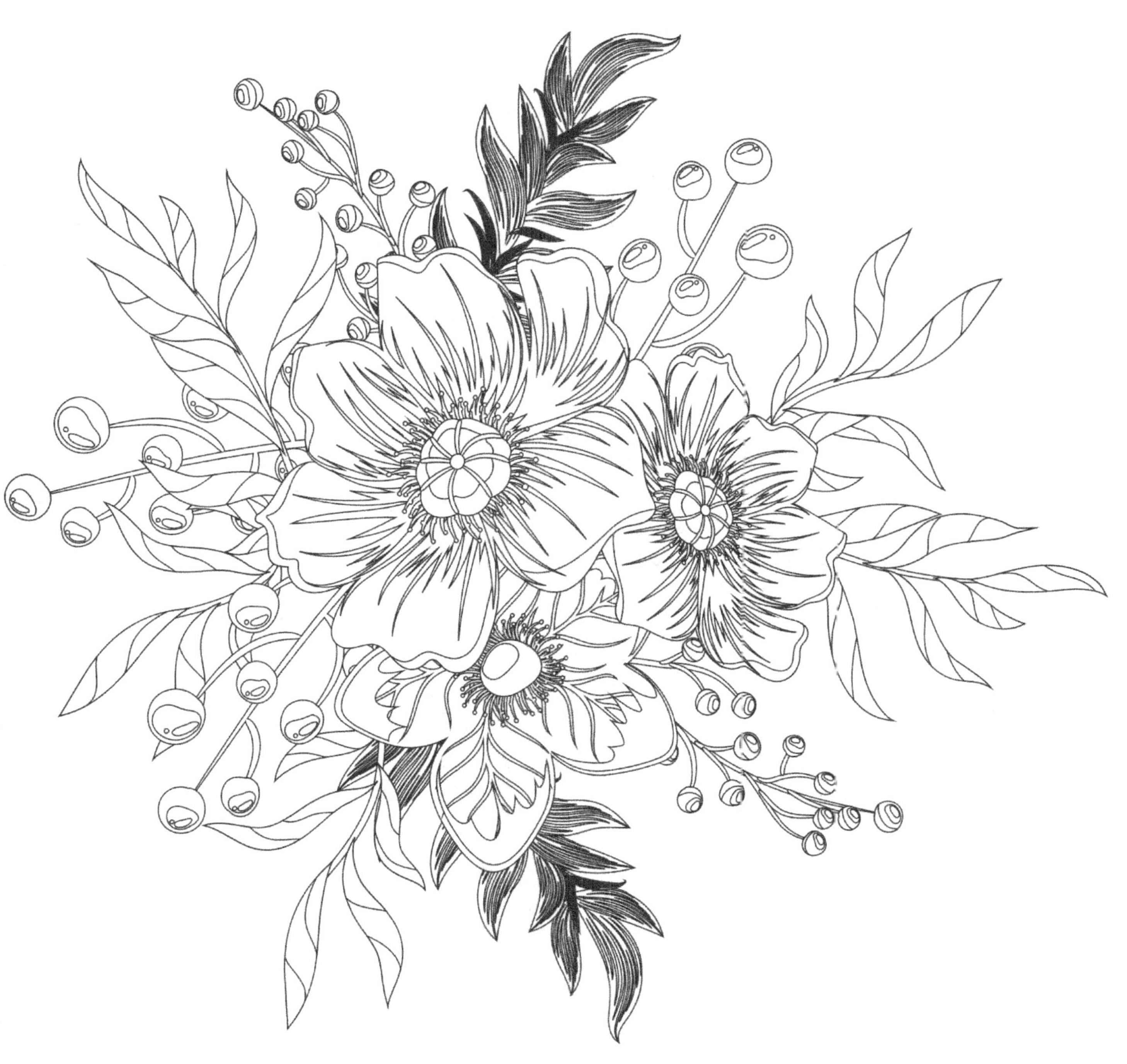

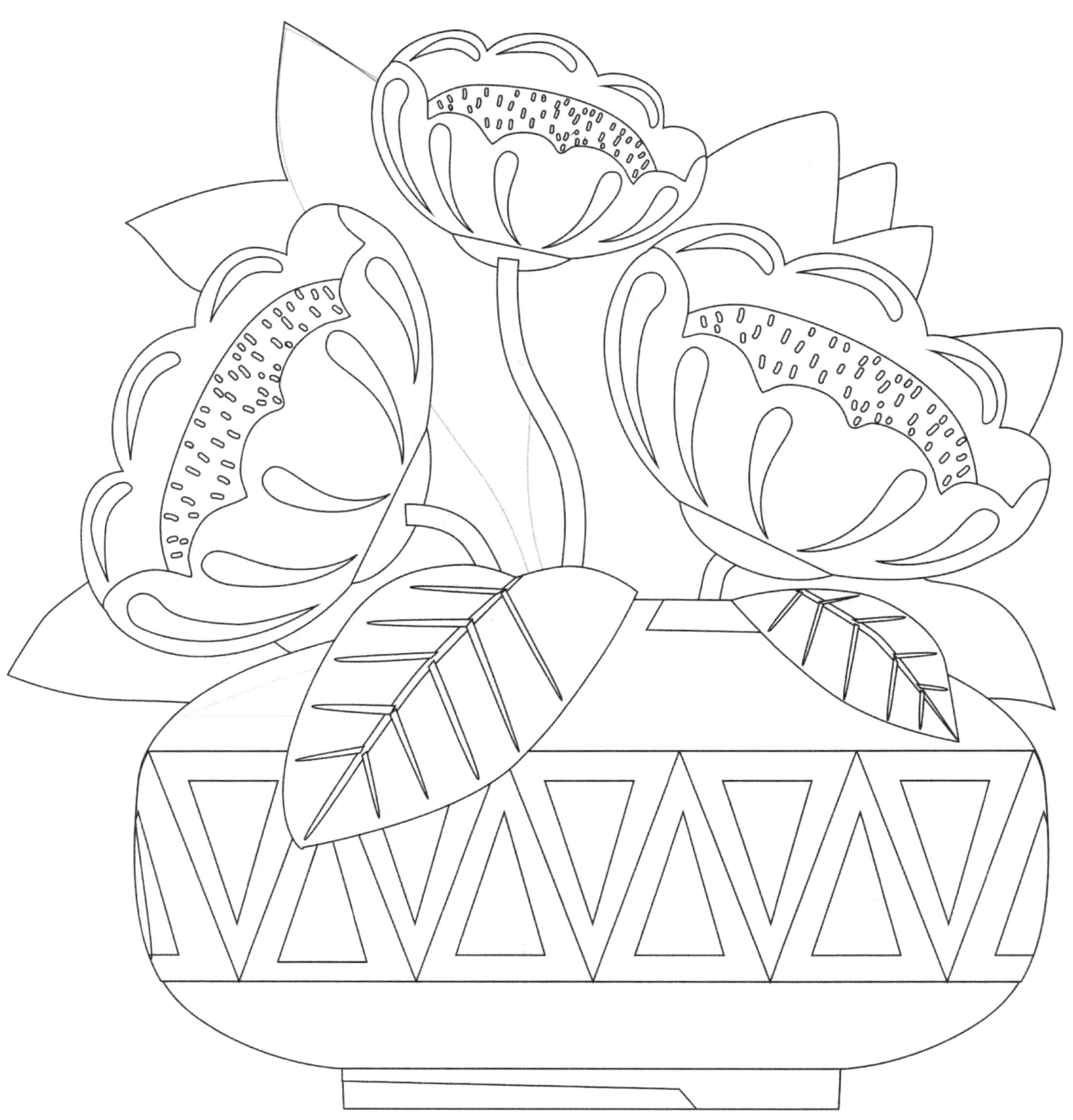

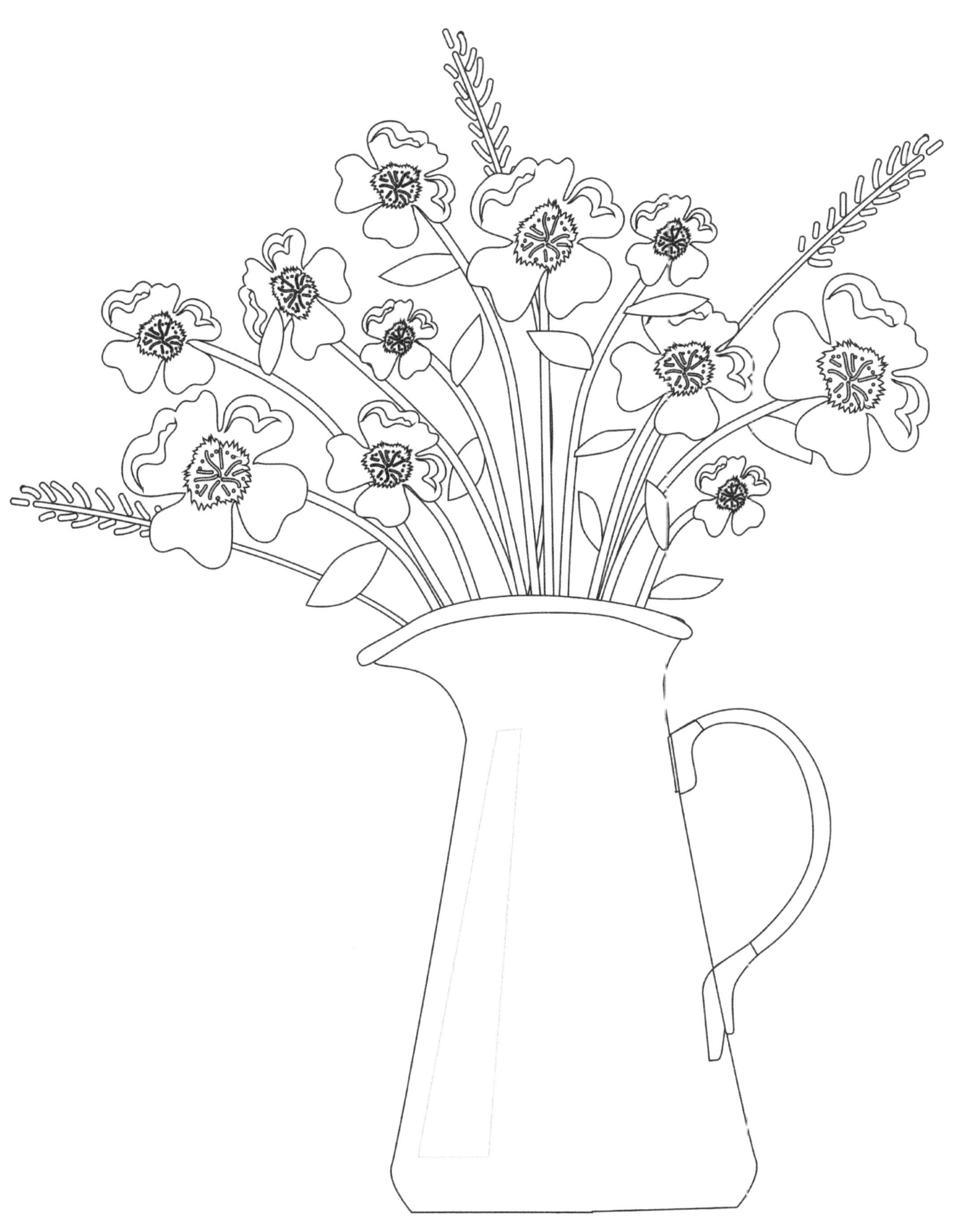

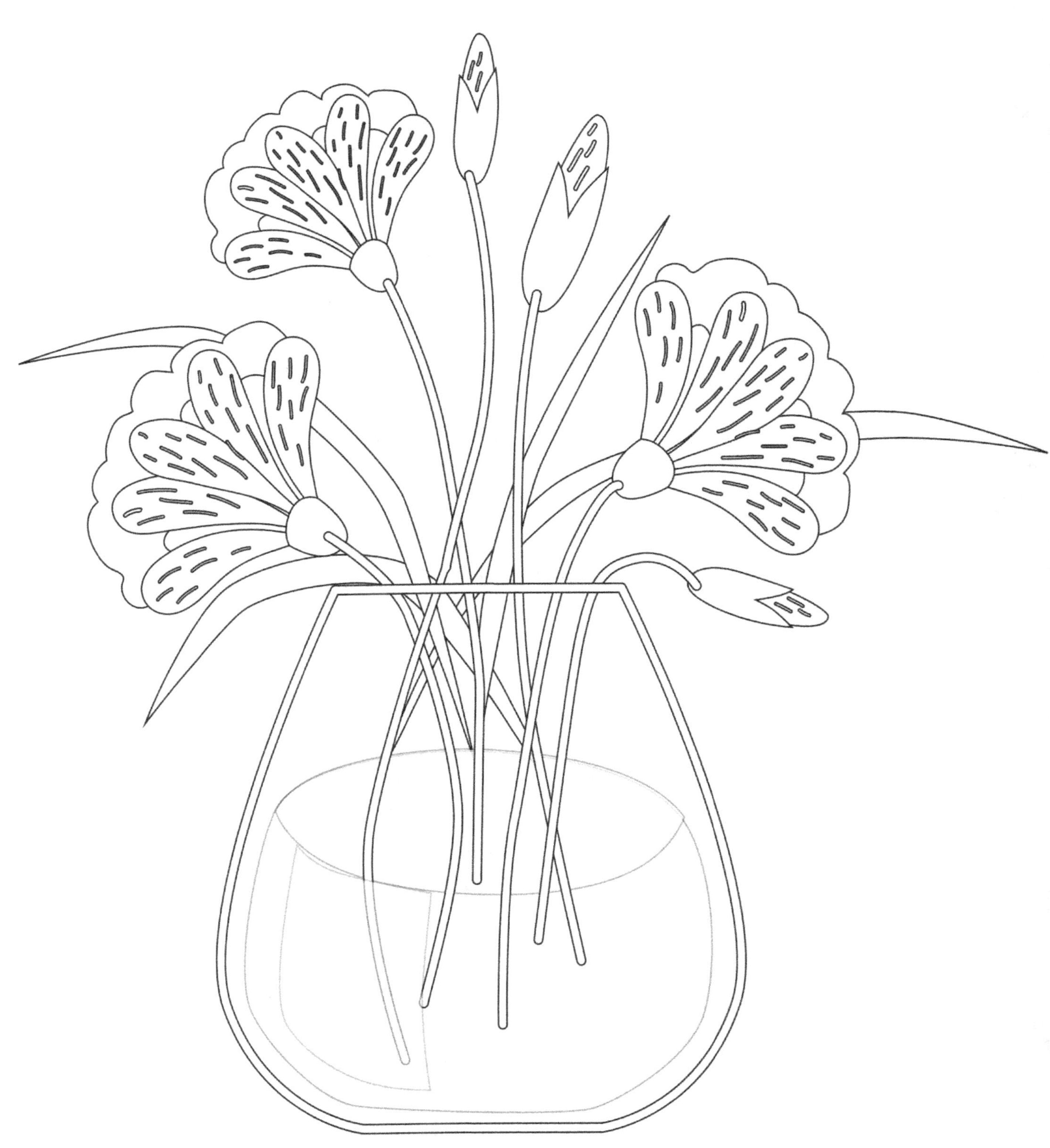

www.ingramcontent.com/pod-product-compliance
Lightning Source LLC
Chambersburg PA
CBHW081432250726
48654CB00013B/1930

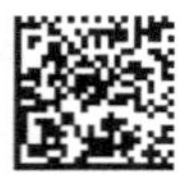